This edition is published by special arrangement with Simon & Schuster Books for Young Readers,
Simon & Schuster Children's Publishing Division.

Grateful acknowledgment is made to Simon & Schuster Books for Young Readers,
Simon & Schuster Children's Publishing Division for permission to reprint
Nature Chains: Butterfly by Moira Butterfield, illustrated by Paul Johnson.
Copyright © 1991 by Teeney Books Limited.

Printed in the United States of America

ISBN   0-15-326531-0

7 8 9 10   179   04

Butterfly

by Moira Butterfield
illustrated by Paul Johnson

Harcourt

Orlando   Boston   Dallas   Chicago   San Diego

Visit *The Learning Site*
www.harcourtschool.com

A female butterfly
lays a clump of eggs
underneath a leaf.

4

The eggs are tiny.
A little caterpillar
grows in each one.

When a caterpillar is ready, it chews a hole in its egg and wriggles out.

It is very hungry.
It munches leaves
and grows bigger.

As the caterpillar grows, its skin gets too tight. The skin splits open.

There is a new skin underneath.

9

The caterpillar's body has lots of little sections in a row. They are called *segments*.

Its legs are good for gripping on to things.

11

When the caterpillar is big enough, it stops eating and settles on a twig or a leaf.

It anchors itself with sticky silk.

The old caterpillar
skin splits open.

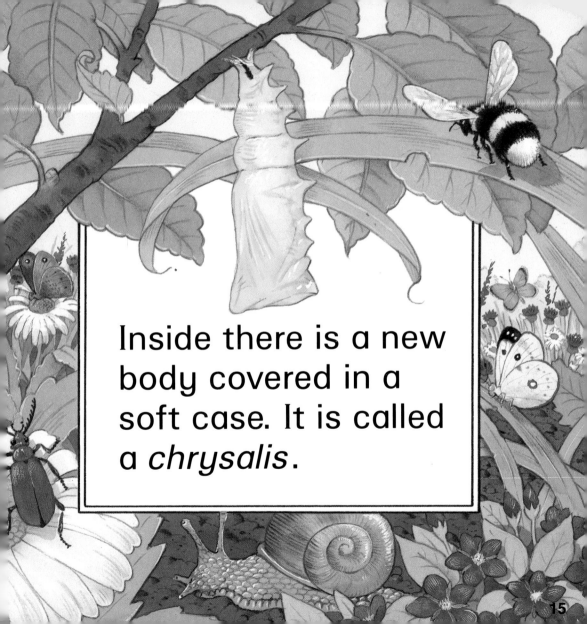

Inside there is a new
body covered in a
soft case. It is called
a *chrysalis*.

A butterfly grows
inside the chrysalis.
When it is ready, it
crawls out.

The new butterfly
sits still for a while,
until it is ready
to fly.

It tries out its wings and lands on a flower. It eats the sugary nectar inside.

One day it may lay eggs of its own, and new caterpillars will start to grow.